Pearson

Year 2

Grammar and Punctuation
Activity Workbook

Author:
Hannah
Hirst-Dunton

Published by Pearson Education Limited, 80 Strand, London, WC2R 0RL.
www.pearsonschools.co.uk

Text © Pearson Education Limited 2021
Edited by Florence Production Ltd
Designed by Pearson Education Limited 2021
Typeset by Florence Production Ltd
Produced by Florence Production Ltd and Sarah Loader
Original illustrations © Pearson Education Limited 2021
Cover design by Pearson Education Limited 2021

The right of Hannah Hirst-Dunton to be identified as author of this work has been asserted by her in accordance with the Copyright, Designs and Patents Act 1988.

First published 2021

24 23 22 21
10 9 8 7 6 5 4 3 2 1

British Library Cataloguing in Publication Data
A catalogue record for this book is available from the British Library

ISBN 978 1 292 42498 9

Copyright notice

Printed in Scotland by Bell & Bain Ltd, Glasgow

Acknowledgements
Front Cover: Neonic Flower/Shutterstock and Sudowoodo/Shutterstock.

The author and publisher would like to thank the following individuals and organisations for permission to reproduce photographs:
Shutterstock: Olga Utchenko iv, 8, 13, 30, 35, 48, 63, 68
All other images © Pearson Education Limited

Notes from the publisher

Contents

About this book

This book will help your child to improve their basic literacy skills, fill gaps in learning and increase confidence in a fun and engaging way. It offers a simple, approachable way for you to guide your child through the grammar and punctuation requirements of the National Curriculum.

Your child's mastery of grammar will allow them to express themselves clearly and meet expectations within the whole English curriculum, and beyond!

Grammar and punctuation made clear

• A **noun phrase** is a group of words that all link to the thing named by the noun. It could be as short as just a determiner and the noun.

Underline the noun phrase in each of the following sentences.

1. <u>Some clouds</u> gather.

2. An aeroplane flew overhead.

3. The sparkling raindrops fall.

4. I put on a bright yellow raincoat.

• This activity book is split into bite-sized, manageable topics that are clearly named.

• Each topic is broken down into a number of sessions that develop particular skills and understanding.

• Every session includes grammar or punctuation guides, which give 'at a glance' guidance.

• Then three activities introduce, practise and reinforce the skill focus.

• Completing all three activities in one sitting will help your child get to grips with the concept.

• There are checkpoints for your child to fill in at the end of each topic. This gives you the chance to see to see where further support is needed.

3 I can form past-tense verbs correctly.

4 I can ensure that verbs agree with subjects and tenses in writing.

5 I know the present-tense and past-tense forms of the verbs 'be' and 'have'.

I know the past-tense ms of some common

How to use this book

- Short sessions work best. Try setting aside half an hour for your child to explore the three activities.

- Try to complete the topics in the given order, as many of them form key foundations for the ones that follow them.

- Your child will ideally work through topics independently, but it's worth being there for when support is needed.

- If your child seems bored or is struggling, suggest they take a break. It might be that they understand the ideas already, or just need time to take something in. They could work on a creative task, such as colouring or following patterns. Try the Pearson Handwriting Activity Workbooks: they contain lots of fun activities, and will also help your child to practise pencil control.

- At the end of a topic, explore the checkpoints with your child and make sure you're happy with what they've understood.

Building from ...
These topics follow on directly from Year 1 to Year 2:

Year 1 topic	Year 2 topic
Nouns	Adjectives Possession
Articles	Determiners
Verbs	Verb forms
Sentences	Conjunctions and clauses
More sentence punctuation	Punctuation
Using 'and'	Conjunctions and clauses

Building towards ...
These topics follow on directly from Year 2 to Year 3:

Year 2 topic	Year 3 topic
More determiners	Demonstratives
Expanded noun phrases	Prepositions
Verb forms	Verb forms
Adverbs	Adverbials
Conjunctions and clauses	Conjunctions and clauses
Punctuation	Direct speech Possession

Getting started

- Make your child's learning space interesting and fun, in a favourite place to sit or with a favourite toy beside them.
- Encourage your child to step away from any technology or energetic games a little while beforehand, and to take some deep breaths to help them focus.
- Make sure they're sitting comfortably at a table and holding their pencil properly.
- Try to sit with your child to start, even if you're occupied with your own task.

A helping hand

Remind your child to ask for help when they need it. In some topics, you may find they need a little extra guidance. Follow the tips below to support them.

Adverbs: What are adverbs? (pages 31–32)

If your child finds adverbs more challenging than adjectives, pull out the verb phrases or adjectival phrases the adverbs create, rather than asking them to look at whole sentences.

For example, pull out 'fell heavily' from 'The snow fell heavily' or 'extremely exciting' from 'Sports day was extremely exciting'.

Emphasise that, like a noun phrase, each of these creates a block of meaning.

Grammar guide

I ran quickly. I was soon exhausted!

- An adverb adds information to a verb or an adject
- Lots of adverbs end '–ly', but not all of them.

Underline the adverbs.

1. Freddie sits neatly.
2. Gran's cat pounces playfully.

Conjunctions and clauses: Using 'and', 'but' and 'because' (pages 36–39) and Using 'or' and 'so' (pages 44–45)

As with using 'and' in Year 1, sometimes it helps to make these exercises practical. You could try writing the pairs of sentences and the conjunctions on slips of paper to be arranged, before asking your child to consider the capital letters and full stops.

Activity 3

Draw lines to show which word would be best to connect each pair of sentences.

Sam washed the car. Megan helped him.

I broke a window. I had to stay at home.

Bella could go out. She could stay in.

I ate lots of breakfast. I was hungry.

or

so

and

but

This can be particularly effective for distinguishing between coordinate and subordinate clauses: swapping the order of a main clause and a subordinate clause will change the meaning of the sentence or make no sense. These 'nonsense' sentences can be quite fun to play with!

Tricky concepts

Determiner phrases

To help your child understand that determiner phrases can be used like single words, try swapping phrases such as 'a few' for single words such as 'some' and then swapping back.

Adding adjectives

When using 'a' or 'an' before an adjective and noun, your child may think about whether the noun, rather than the adjective, begins with a consonant or vowel. Encourage them to say the phrase aloud and focus on the sound that follows the article.

Possessive apostrophes

Your child may struggle with the fact that apostrophes are used in possessive nouns but not possessive pronouns. Simple practice is often the best way to overcome misconceptions like this.

Technical terms

Even when children know and understand the structures of grammar, terminology can make things seem difficult. Help your child to use the Glossary, which makes the terms clearer.

Progress check

- Once your child has worked on some activities, judge how confident they are with carrying on alone. If they're keen for independence, they're probably on the right track.
- Encourage your child to talk to you about what they are learning. Getting an explanation in their own words will show you how much they've understood.

Extension activities

- The National Curriculum for Composition suggests that children note down key words and phrases to use in creative writing. Challenge them to include detailed noun phrases and effective adverbs.
- After your child completes the creative writing project, discuss the effects of the noun phrases and adverbs they have included. Explore the effects of changing these words while the rest of the sentences stay the same.

Putting grammar and punctuation skills to use

Help your child to understand that their new grammar and punctuation skills are in use everywhere. Encourage them to find examples around them, including in their reading materials.

- When your child is reading poetry, draw particular attention to use of adjectives and adverbs.
- In non-fiction texts, draw attention to the use of Standard English.

1: What are determiners?

Activity 1

Grammar guide

- Determiners come before nouns.
- Articles are a type of determiner.
- The words 'a', 'an', 'the' and 'some' are articles.

> I went to see **<u>a</u>** painting at **<u>an</u>** art gallery with **<u>some</u>** friends. **<u>The</u>** painting was very famous.

- Use '**a**' or '**an**' when you talk about any singular thing.
- Use '**an**' before a vowel sound and '**a**' before a consonant sound.
- Use '**some**' when you talk about any plural thing.
- Use '**the**' when you talk about a particular thing or things, singular or plural.

> Circle the articles that are used incorrectly. Say what would be the correct article in each case. The first one has been done for you.

> I went out at (some) weekend. I went to a theme park. It was the great day out. I went with some friends. Some best ride was called 'Speed Spinner'. It was a enormous rollercoaster.

Activity 2

Grammar guide

> The display shows **many** labels, **two** poems, **a lot of** key words and **plenty of** pictures.

- Not all determiners are articles. Other words can give information about nouns, too.
- Determiners can be **single words** or **more than one word**.

Underline all of the determiners. The first one has been done for you.

Asa and I were taking <u>some</u> boxes out of the attic. We opened most of the boxes. Inside, we found many forgotten things. There were several old photos and a few letters. There was also one dusty box we could not open, although we tried all the keys.

Activity 3

Write down the determiners that you underlined in Activity 2. Write what information each determiner adds. Use the words below. The first one has been done for you.

general	particular	plural	singular

some – general, plural

_____   _____

_____   _____

_____   _____

2: Adding information about number

Activity 1

- Determiners can give information about number.

Choose one of the following determiners to complete each sentence. Use each word only once. The first one has been done for you.

| some | no | most | one |

1 Fred ate _____ some _____ vegetables.

2 We enjoy _____ films.

3 I was only _____ minute late!

4 Nia was hungry, but there were

_____ cakes left.

Activity 2

- Determiners can be single words or more than one word.

Complete this story using determiners that add information about number. The first one has been done for you.

Ida was in _____ an _____ ice cream shop.

She looked at _____ flavours.

'Can I have _____ kind?' she asked.

'You can choose _____ scoops,' said Mum.

Activity 3

Write two or three sentences about things you might have on your desk. Use all the determiners below. Use each determiner only once.

every	plenty of	five

_____

_____

_____

_____

3: Choosing determiners

Activity 1

Grammar guide

- Determiners can give information about number.
- They can be single words or more than one word.
- They can include articles.

Determiners

| a | most | all three | one |

| some | a few of the | many |

Choose one of the determiners above to complete each sentence. Use a different determiner for each sentence. The first one has been done for you.

1 Joshua scored ____a few of the____ goals on Saturday.

2 There was _____ newspaper left to deliver.

3 It rained on _____ days of our holiday.

Activity 2

Look again at the determiners given in Activity 1. Choose two determiners that match each description. Use each determiner only once. The first one has been done for you.

1 There is a single thing.

_____a_____   _____one_____

2 There is more than one thing.

_____   _____

3 There is more than one thing, but not all of them are needed.

_____   _____

Activity 3

Write two sentences about what pupils in your class like to do. Use at least three different determiners.

_____

_____

_____

_____

What do I Know?

1. I know what determiners are.

2. I know that determiners can give basic information about number.

3. I know that determiners can show whether something is general or particular.

4. I can use determiners to give information about number.

1: What are adjectives?

Activity 1

Grammar guide

The **bright** **sun** shines. A **beautiful** **butterfly** flutters.

- **Describing words** can be added before **nouns**. These describing words are called adjectives.
- Adjectives add information to the nouns. They describe the thing, person, event or idea named.

Circle all the adjectives in these sentences.

My (best) friend's birthday is on Sunday.

He will have a big party in his garden.

His older sister is baking him a delicious cake with blue icing.

Activity 2

Grammar guide

This is **a short** test. It is **an important** test.
I got **some new** paper. I wrote **the right** answers.

- **Determiners** come before **adjectives**.
- Use 'an' before a vowel sound at the start of the adjective.
- Use 'a' before a consonant sound.

Complete each of these sentences by adding a determiner and an adjective.

1 _____A tall_____ woman stepped off the train.

2 She was carrying _____ suitcases.

3 _____ car was waiting for her.

4 _____ driver opened the door.

Activity 3

Write two sentences describing what you look like. Use at least one adjective in each sentence.

I have _____

_____

_____

2: Expanding noun phrases

Activity 1

Grammar guide

> **The tree** is tall. **The green leaves** grow.

- A phrase is a group of words that means one thing. It could be as short as two words.
- A **noun phrase** is a group of words that all link to the thing named by the noun. It could be as short as just a determiner and the noun.

> Underline the noun phrase in each of the following sentences.

1. <u>Some clouds</u> gather.

2. An aeroplane flew overhead.

3. The sparkling raindrops fall.

4. I put on a bright yellow raincoat.

Activity 2

Grammar guide

> **The tree** is tall. **The green leaves** grow.

- A **simple noun phrase** is just two words that name one thing: a determiner and a noun.
- Adding an <u>adjective</u> to a simple noun phrase makes it bigger and more detailed. The phrase becomes an **expanded noun phrase**.

Write two short sentences about a perfect day. Include at least one expanded noun phrase in each sentence.

On a perfect day, I _____

_____

_____

Activity 3

Write down each expanded noun phrase you used in Activity 2. Then underline all the adjectives you have used.

a <u>perfect</u> day _____

_____

_____

What do I Know?

1 I know what an adjective is.

2 I can spot an adjective.

3 I know where to place an adjective.

4 I can use adjectives in my writing.

5 I can spot a noun phrase.

6 I know that adjectives can be used to expand noun phrases.

7 I can write sentences using expanded noun phrases.

1: Practising the present tense

Activity 1

Grammar guide

> I **watch** the bird. **Nia watches** the bird. **We watch** it together.
> I **move** forward. The **bird moves** away. **We move** back again.

- <u>Who or what</u> does the action can change a **verb**.
- <u>When</u> the action happens can also change a **verb**.
- If the action happens now, the verb is in the present tense.
- If a present-tense verb has '**I**', '**you**', a **plural pronou**n or a plural noun before it, do **not** add '<u>s</u>' or '<u>es</u>' at the end.
- If a verb has a **singular noun** before it, add '<u>s</u>' or '<u>es</u>' at the end.
- Add '<u>es</u>' rather than '<u>s</u>' to verbs ending '**ch**', '**sh**', '**x**', '**zz**' or '**s**'.

Rewrite these sentences, correcting the verbs.

I plays outside. Then the weather getes gloomy. We watches TV instead.

I play outside.

Activity 2

Grammar guide

I **go** home. I **hurry** upstairs. I **obey** the rule about bedtime.
My brother **goes** home. My brother **hurries** upstairs.
My brother **obeys** the rule about bedtime.

- For **a present-tense verb ending 'o'**, usually add 'es'.
- For **a present-tense verb ending in a consonant and then 'y'**, change the 'y' to 'ies'.
- However, for **a present-tense verb ending in a vowel and then 'y'**, simply add 's'.

Complete these present-tense sentences to show how the verbs change.

1 I cycle home. My sister _____cycles_____ home with me.

2 I carry one bag. Ken _____ the other.

3 We cross the road. Oma _____ the road, too.

4 I do my homework. Cara _____ her homework as well.

Activity 3

Underline one word to make each sentence correct.

1 The little baby **crys / cries / cryes**.

2 The toy car **gos / gies / goes**.

3 Margaret **plays / plaies / playes**.

2: What is the past tense?

Activity 1

Grammar guide

> I **want** an ice cream. **Kerri wants** one, too. **We walk** to the shop.
> I **wanted** an ice cream. **Kerri wanted** one, too. **We walked** to the shop.

- Verbs can change depending on when the action happens.
- If the action happens now, the verb is in the **present tense**.
- If the action has already happened, the verb is in the **past tense**.
- Many past-tense verbs can be formed by adding the suffix 'ed'.
- Past-tense verbs do **not** change depending on **who does the action**.

Underline the past-tense verbs. Circle the present-tense verbs.

Mandip played video games when he finished his chores. I enjoy video games, too.

I cleaned my room. I fold my clothes.
I want my turn with the game!

Activity 2

Grammar guide

We **bake** bread and cake. We **try** them. We **enjoy** the bread. We **prefer** the cake.

We **baked** bread and cake. We **tried** them. We **enjoyed** the bread. We **preferred** the cake.

Here are some more rules for forming past-tense verbs.

- **If the verb ends in 'e', add just 'd'.**
- **If the verb ends in a consonant and then 'y', change the 'y' to 'i' before adding 'ed'.**
- **However, if the verb ends in a vowel and then 'y', just add 'ed'.**
- **If a verb ends in one vowel and then one consonant (not 'y'), usually double the consonant and add 'ed'.**

Tick the past-tense sentences.

We tidied up.	✓	Snow delays the train.	◻
Dana travelled to the city.	◻	I stayed at home.	◻
I try some fruit.	◻	Una claps.	◻

Activity 3

Tick the sentences with correct past-tense verbs.

I carryed my chair.	◻	Tim likeed Shona.	◻
We planned a school trip.	◻	You enjoyed the concert.	◻
The driver stoped the bus.	◻		

3: Using the past tense

Activity 1

Grammar guide

- Verbs can change depending on when the action happens.
- If the action happens now, the verb is in the **present tense**.
- If the action has already happened, the verb is in the **past tense**.
- Many past-tense verbs can be formed by adding 'ed' at the end.

Add 'ed' to create past-tense verbs from these present-tense verbs.

1 cover _____ *covered* _____

2 ask _____

3 help _____

Activity 2

Grammar guide

- If a verb already ends in 'e', add just 'd'.
- If a verb ends in a consonant and then 'y', change the 'y' to 'i' before adding 'ed'.
- However, for a verb ending in a vowel and then 'y', add 'ed'.
- If a verb ends in a single vowel and then a consonant other than 'y', usually double the consonant before adding 'ed'.
- Past-tense verbs do **not** change depending on who does the action.

Complete the table with the correct past-tense form of each verb.

Singular		Plural	
Present tense	**Past tense**	**Present tense**	**Past tense**
I look.		They spy.	
You stare.		We travel.	
He watches.		You stay.	

Activity 3

Write two sentences about what you did yesterday.
Use past-tense forms of some of these verbs.

look listen play wait

enjoy use try

_____

_____

_____

_____

4: What is verb agreement?

Activity 1

Grammar guide

- Verbs can change to show when the action happens – the tense.
- Present-tense verbs can also change depending on their subject: the person or thing doing the action.
- Verbs must match their subject and the tense of their sentence.
- This matching is called verb agreement.

Rewrite each sentence and correct the verb.

1 Ella and Tom plays football.

_____

2 For my party, Mum books a magician.

_____

Activity 2

Circle the verbs that do not agree with their subject or are in the wrong tense.

Last term, Harriet and I start a board games club at school. We share our favourite games, and tried some new ones. Now, more students played. They enjoys board games, too. The games are really popular!

Write the incorrect verbs in the first column of the table.
Then write the correct verb forms in the second column.

	What are the incorrect verbs?	What are the correct verb forms?
Verb 1:	start	
Verb 2:		
Verb 3:		
Verb 4:		

Activity 3

Complete the sentences using the correct forms of some of these verbs.

want   help   play   paint

annoy   like   hurry

1 Last week, Tara and David ____played football____.

2 Every day, Martha _____.

3 They often _____.

4 Last year, I _____.

5: Understanding 'be' and 'have'

Activity 1

Complete the tables with the correct verb forms.

HAVE	Present tense	Past tense
I	have	
you		
he		
we		
you		
they		

BE	Present tense	Past tense
I	am	
you		
he		
we		
you		
they		

Activity 2

1 Fill in the gaps with the right present-tense forms of the verb 'have'.

Every night, I ___have___ the same dream. You _____ a box with two big locks. Your brother _____ the keys. We _____ a race to get them. Then we see that they _____ broken ends and can't be used.

2 Fill in the gaps with the right past-tense forms of the verb 'be'.

We ___were___ all in the school play. The setting _____ a dangerous city. Pete _____ the thief and he robbed a bank. You _____ the manager and Jamala _____ a police officer. The other pupils _____ citizens. I _____ the detective and I stopped the thief. You _____ all very grateful.

Activity 3

1 Look again at the story in Activity 2, question 1. Say the story in the past tense.

2 Look again at the story in Activity 2, question 2. Say the story in the present tense.

6: Understanding other irregular verbs

Activity 1

Grammar guide

- Irregular verbs do not follow rules.
- Lots of verbs have irregular past tenses. These have to be learned.
- They must still match their subject (who or what does the action).
- They must still match their tense (when the action happens).

Complete the tables by writing the present-tense version of each irregular past-tense verb.

Present tense	Past tense
I write.	I wrote .
She	She felt.

Present tense	Past tense
I	I grew .
It	It found.

Activity 2

Complete the tables by writing the irregular past-tense version of each present-tense verb.

Singular		Plural	
Present tense	**Past tense**	**Present tense**	**Past tense**
I say.	I said.	We come.	We
You go.	You	You see.	You
He takes.	He	They know.	They

Singular			Plural		
Present tense	**Past tense**		**Present tense**	**Past tense**	
I get.	I		We think.	We	
You give.	You		You tell.	You	
She runs.	He		They can.	They	

Activity 3

Change the verbs to put the story into the past tense.

The pupils begin their lesson today with a song. They sing together and then they read. They speak about their books and they make sure that they understand the topic.

The pupils _____ their lesson today with a song.

They _____ together and then they _____ .

They _____ about their books and they _____

sure that they _____ the topic.

7: What are progressive verbs?

Activity 1

Grammar guide

> I sing. I **am** *singing*. I **was** *singing*.
> You sing. You **are** *singing*. You **were** *singing*.
> She sings. She **is** *singing*. She **was** *singing*.

- Progressive verbs are used to describe events that continue, or 'progress', over a period of time.
- They are created using two verbs. The verb that names the action ends in '-ing'. This is called the **present participle**.
- A helper verb comes before it. This is called an **auxiliary verb**.
- The progressive tense is formed with the **auxiliary verb 'be'**.

> Circle the auxiliary verbs. Underline the present participles.

1 I (am) going to the ice rink.

2 The cat is pouncing on the light beams.

3 Caris was feeling better.

4 We were relaxing in the sunshine.

Activity 2

Grammar guide

I sing. I **am** singing. I **was** singing.

- Present-progressive verbs use the **present form of the auxiliary verb**.
- Past-progressive verbs use the **past form of the auxiliary verb**.

Tick the sentences that use progressive verbs correctly. Underline the mistakes in the other sentences.

1 Anima was not expecting to win, but hoped she would. ✓

2 We are <u>wait</u> for the train, but it's late. ☐

3 They are travelling abroad until the end of the year. ☐

4 Geese had flying low over the meadow when I looked up. ☐

5 Lexi was getting annoyed by Jess's bad memory. ☐

6 Mum coming to collect you, but there's a traffic jam. ☐

Activity 3

Draw lines to match each sentence to its tense.

Anita's jeans were wearing out.

Josef's rucksack is too heavy.

The fair was open all summer.

Despite the snow, trains are running.

simple past

present progressive

past progressive

simple present

8: Using progressive verbs

Activity 1

Grammar guide

- Progressive verbs are formed from the auxiliary verb 'to be' and a present participle (a verb ending '–ing').
- Past-progressive verbs use the past form of the auxiliary verb ('was' or 'were').
- Present-progressive verbs use the present form of the auxiliary verb ('am', 'are' or 'is').

> Fill the gaps with the correct forms of the verb 'be'.

1 Yesterday, I _____ travelling for a long time.

2 At the moment, Mathias _____ waiting for his friend.

3 Last month, you _____ training to run a race.

4 Today, I _____ wearing a hat I made myself.

Activity 2

1 Rewrite the sentences as past-progressive sentences.

a Tara ate in the cafeteria.

    Tara was eating in the cafeteria.

b Jon and I kicked the ball to each other during break.

_____

c I looked everywhere for my school bag.

_____

2 Rewrite the sentences as present-progressive sentences.

a Channel 19 shows my favourite programme today.

_____

b I cook dinner with Uncle Aarav.

_____

Activity 3

Underline the verbs that should be corrected to progressive forms.

Marc and I <u>help</u> to set up our friend Lottie's party when I got a phone call.

It was Lottie. "I run late!" she said.

"Don't worry," I told her. "I wait to greet people for you."

When she arrived, everyone had a great time already and looked forward to trying her cake.

What do I Know?

1 I can form singular and plural present-tense verbs.

2 I know what the past tense is.

3 I can form past-tense verbs correctly.

4 I can ensure that verbs agree with subjects and tenses in writing.

5 I know the present-tense and past-tense forms of the verbs 'be' and 'have'.

6 I know the past-tense forms of some common irregular verbs.

7 I know what progressive tenses are.

8 I can form present-progressive and past-progressive verbs.

1: What are adverbs?

Activity 1

Grammar guide

I **ran** quick<u>ly</u>. I was **soon** **exhausted**!

- An **adverb** adds information to a **verb** or an **adjective**.
- Lots of adverbs end '–<u>ly</u>', but not all of them.

Underline the adverbs.

1. Freddie sits <u>neatly</u>.

2. Gran's cat pounces playfully.

3. I learned lots today.

4. They shouted loudly.

5. She played outside.

Activity 2

Underline the adverb in each of the following sentences. Write 'verb' or 'adjective' to show the kind of word the adverb is giving information about.

1 The snow fell <u>heavily</u>. _____verb_____

2 Sports day was extremely exciting. _____

3 I'll see you later. _____

4 It's so cold! _____

5 Kim almost finished her book. _____

Activity 3

Tick the sentences that contain adverbs.

It's a lovely surprise! ☐

What happens next? ☐

Climbing is a dangerous activity. ☐

We cross the road carefully. ☐

Afterwards, Jo sadly left. ☐

2: Adding adverbs

Activity 1

> **Grammar guide**
>
> - An **adverb** adds information to a **verb** or an **adjective**.

> Add one of these adverbs to complete each sentence.

| suddenly | happily | kindly | finally | yesterday |

1. The fox appeared ___suddenly___ .

2. Miguel _____ helped his gran.

3. The woman smiled _____ .

Activity 2

> Add one of these adverbs to each sentence. Then say your new sentence out loud.

| now | loudly | next | today |

| slowly | badly | well | soon |

1. I answer the question. ___well___

2. We play football. _____

3. I have a maths lesson. _____

4. We have some free time. _____

Activity 3

Add an adverb of your own to the following sentences.

1 The garden is untidy.

_____

2 Are you leaving?

_____

3 Kaito tidied his room.

_____

What do I know?

1 I know what an adverb is.

2 I can spot an adverb in a sentence.

3 I can choose an adverb and add it to a sentence.

Conjunctions and clauses

1: Practising 'and'

Activity 1

> I took my hat. I hurried outside.
> I took my hat **and** I hurried outside.

- Sentences can be linked to form longer sentences.
- The **original sentences** become **clauses** in the new sentence.
- The word '**and**' can link two clauses to form one sentence.
- Linking words such as 'and' are called conjunctions.

Link each pair of clauses using 'and'.

1 We played games. Then we watched a film.

We played games and then we watched a film.

2 I went sledging. Hoonie came with me.

_____

3 I've always wanted a pet. Soon I'll get one.

_____

Activity 2

1 Say two sentences about two things that you like to eat. Write them as one sentence, using 'and'.

_____

_____

2 Say two sentences about two activities you enjoy. Write them as one sentence, using 'and'.

_____

_____

3 Say two sentences about two things you did recently. Write them as one sentence, using 'and'.

_____

_____

Activity 3

Look again at your answers to Activity 2. Circle the conjunctions. Then underline each clause that you wrote.

2: Understanding 'but' and 'because'

Activity 1

Grammar guide

It is raining. It is warm. **It is raining but it is warm.**
I use an umbrella. It is raining. **I use an umbrella because it is raining.**

- **Conjunctions** link sentences to form one longer sentence.
- The word 'and' is a conjunction.
- The words '**but**' and '**because**' are also **conjunctions**.
- The **original sentences** become **clauses** in the new sentence.

Underline the word that links each pair of sentences.

1. The fox slept outside. The cat slept inside.
The fox slept outside but the cat slept inside.

2. Kerri hurries. She is late.
Kerri hurries because she is late.

Activity 2

Grammar guide

The bud opens **and** the flower blooms.
The flower blooms **but** the leaves wilt.
The flower blooms **because** the sun shines.

- The word '**and**' links similar ideas.
- The word '**but**' links different ideas that could be compared.
- The word '**because**' comes before a reason.

Tick one box to show what each conjunction tells you.

1 Mary stays inside <u>because</u> it is raining.

These are similar ideas. ☐
These are different ideas. ☐
The second idea is a reason. ☐

2 The sun is shining <u>and</u> the beach is warm.

These are similar ideas. ☐
These are different ideas. ☐
The second idea is a reason. ☐

3 The weather is windy <u>but</u> my kite will not fly.

These are similar ideas. ☐
These are different ideas. ☐
The second idea is a reason. ☐

Activity 3

Tick the sentences that use 'and', 'but' and 'because' correctly.

The old man yawns because he feels sleepy. ☐

Yan tried to see but it was too dark. ☐

It's sunny because I have to stay in the classroom. ☐

Aunt Tabby cooked and I helped her. ☐

We met up but we went to the park. ☐

3: Using 'and', 'but' and 'because'

Activity 1

Grammar guide

- Sentences can be linked to form one longer sentence.
- The words 'and', 'but' and 'because' can link sentences.
- The word 'and' links similar ideas.
- The word 'but' links different ideas that could be compared.
- The word 'because' comes before a reason.

1 Which word should come before a reason?

because

2 Which word would you use to link two different ideas?

3 Which word would you use to link two similar ideas?

Activity 2

1 Say two sentences that describe an event and the reason it happened. Then write them as one sentence, using 'because'.

_____

_____

_____

2 Say two sentences that contain two contrasting ideas. Then write them as one sentence, using 'but'.

_____

_____

_____

Activity 3

Add the correct conjunction to link each pair of clauses.

1 My feet hurt _____ I have walked a long way.

2 I want to go out _____ I have to finish my homework.

3 Nana kicks the ball to me _____ I kick it back.

4: Understanding 'or' and 'so'

Activity 1

Grammar guide

> It is raining. It is sunny. It is raining **or** it is sunny.
> It is raining. I use an umbrella. It is raining **so** I use an umbrella.

- **Conjunctions** link sentences to form one longer sentence.
- The **original sentences** become **clauses** in the new sentence.
- The words '**or**' and '**so**' are two more **conjunctions**.

Underline the conjunctions.

> I wanted to go out <u>because</u> it was warm. I called my friend and I grabbed my frisbee. We could go to the park or we could play in the garden. We chose the park but that was a mistake. It was a Saturday so the park was crowded. We left because we could not play.

Activity 2

Grammar guide

> It is raining **or** it is sunny.
> It is raining **so** I use an umbrella.

- The word '**or**' links two possible things. Only one of them can happen or be true.
- The word '**so**' introduces an effect.

Draw lines to show what each conjunction tells you.

Bill was early but Elli was late.

I play with Salib or I play with Jess.

Dad was annoyed because the train was late.

I felt ill so we went to see the doctor.

Nish reads his book and he enjoys it.

The second idea is an effect.

These are similar ideas.

These are very different ideas.

The second idea is a reason.

There are two possibilities.

Activity 3

Underline the **correct** conjunction in each sentence.

1 I will wear a coat **so / or** I will be cold.

2 Sophie could jog in the park **so / or** she could cycle there.

3 Darren picked up the baby **so / or** she stopped crying.

4 We went to the cinema **so / or** we could watch a film.

5: Using 'or' and 'so'
Activity 1

- Conjunctions link sentences to form one longer sentence.
- The words 'or' and 'so' are conjunctions.
- The word 'or' links two possible things. Only one of them can happen or be true.
- The word 'so' introduces an effect.

1 Link this pair of sentences using 'so'.

I missed my gran. I went to visit her.

I missed my gran

2 Link this pair of sentences using 'or'.

We can go swimming. We can play mini golf.

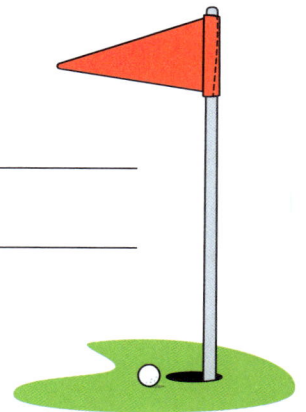

Activity 2

1 Say two sentences that describe two possible games you could play. Write them as one sentence, using 'or'.

We could play _____

_____

2 Say a sentence describing the weather. Say another sentence describing the effect of that weather on what you can do. Write them as one sentence, using 'so'.

_____

_____

Activity 3

Draw lines to show which word would be best to connect each pair of sentences.

Sam washed the car. Megan helped him.	or
I broke a window. I had to stay at home.	so
Bella could go out. She could stay in.	and
I ate lots of breakfast. I was hungry.	but
The sun is out. The wind is cold.	because

6: Different types of clause

Activity 1

Grammar guide

The weather looks stormy so Achak stays inside.

- Sentences can become underline{clauses} in part of a longer sentence.
- Clauses, like sentences, need a **subject** and a **verb**.

Underline the clauses below. How many are there?

I couldn't find my shoes so I'm late for school. I hurry but I feel bad because I was late last week, too. I'm worried. Will people be cross or will they laugh? I run in and I apologise.

Activity 2

Grammar guide

It is bright but it was cold. It was cold but it is bright.

- A **main clause** gives a main point in a sentence. A sentence can include more than one **main** clause.
- Swapping the order of two **main clauses** does not affect the meaning of a sentence.

It was late so I went to bed. I went to bed so it was late.

A **subordinate clause** gives extra information.
Swapping a **main clause** and a **subordinate clause** does affect the meaning of a sentence, or makes no sense.

1 Tick the sentences that include subordinate clauses.

- We went to a theme park because it was my birthday. ☑
- We could go on rides or we could see a music show. ☐
- We got there early so the queues were short. ☐
- The shop was big and it was crowded. ☐
- The day out was exhausting but I loved it! ☐

2 Write a short sentence containing a main clause and a subordinate clause, using 'so'.

_____

_____

Activity 3

Grammar guide

It was bright **but** it was cold. The snow fell **so** I made a snowman.

- A **coordinating conjunction** links main clauses. The words 'and', 'but' and 'or' are coordinating conjunctions.
- A **subordinating conjunction** introduces a subordinate clause. The words 'because' and 'so' are subordinating conjunctions.

Circle the subordinating conjunctions.

and   but   because   so   or

What do I Know?

1. I can use the conjunction 'and' to link clauses in a sentence.

2. I understand the meanings of 'but' and 'because'.

3. I can choose 'and', 'but' or 'because' to connect two ideas.

4. I can say and then write sentences using 'because' and 'but'.

5. I understand the meanings of 'or' and 'so'.

6. I can choose 'or' or 'so' to connect two ideas.

7. I can say and then write sentences using 'or' and 'so'.

8. I know what main clauses and subordinate clauses are.

9. I can write sentences that include coordinating and subordinating conjunctions.

1: Practising sentence punctuation

Activity 1

Punctuation guide

This is heavy. Could you come and help me? Hurry up!

- A **statement** gives a piece of information. It ends in a **full stop**.
- A **question** asks for information. It ends with a **question mark**.
- An **exclamation** is cried or shouted suddenly. It could express surprise, pain or strong emotion. It ends with an **exclamation mark**.

Label each sentence as a statement, a question or an exclamation. Circle the punctuation mark that helped you to decide.

1 Do you think people will use flying cars in the future⟨?⟩

＿＿＿question＿＿＿＿＿＿

2 Get away from that pylon!

＿＿＿＿＿＿＿＿＿＿＿

3 When I grow up, I want to be a pilot.

＿＿＿＿＿＿＿＿＿＿＿

Activity 2

1 Write a statement of your own. Make sure you punctuate it correctly.

_____

_____

2 Write a question of your own. Make sure you punctuate it correctly.

_____

_____

3 Write an exclamation of your own. Make sure you punctuate it correctly.

_____

_____

Activity 3

Rewrite the second statement below as a similar question and exclamation. Think about how the words change as well as how the punctuation changes.

Statement	We should slow down.	You can help me.
Question	Should we slow down?	
Exclamation	Slow down!	

2: Understanding lists

Activity 1

Punctuation guide

In the pond, there are **fish**, **frogs**, **newts** and **insects**.

- A list is a series of connected things.

Read the sentences below. What things did Li-An look at? Write four nouns.

Li-An lay on the grass. She looked at the trees, the birds, the bees and the clouds above.

Noun 1   _trees_

Noun 2   _____

Noun 3   _____

Noun 4   _____

Activity 2

Punctuation guide

In the pond, there are **fish**, **frogs**, **newts** and **insects**.

- Most **items** in a list are separated by **commas**.
- The last two items in a list are connected with '**and**', not separated with a comma.

Tick the sentences that contain correctly formed lists.

Carole likes Maths Drama and PE. ☐

Get out the milk, eggs, flour and butter. ☑

We need tomatoes, onions, potatoes, carrots. ☐

Fruit, vegetables and water are good for you. ☐

Hillie ran in the sun, the rain, and the snow. ☐

Activity 3

Tick the sentences that include lists.

I grabbed my coat and my bag and hurried to school. ☐

Suddenly, Kaymar and Sunitra shouted out to me. ☐

You need to walk, feed and brush your puppy. ☐

Dad baked cookies, scones, cupcakes and muffins. ☐

Aunt May and I worked on art projects. ☐

3: Writing lists

Activity 1

Punctuation guide

- A list is a series of connected things.

Complete the list sentence using this information.

Kim has his coat. Kim has his scarf. Kim has his gloves.

Kim has his _____coat_____, _____

and _____.

Activity 2

Punctuation guide

- Most items in a list are separated by commas.
- The last two items in a list are connected with 'and', not separated with a comma.

Complete each sentence with a list of three nouns or noun phrases.

1 Outside the window, Margie saw

a tree _____ , _____

and _____

2 Under his bed, Tom kept

_____ , _____

and _____

3 Naja's favourite animals were

_____ , _____

and _____

Activity 3

Write a list sentence about four things you ate yesterday.

I ate _____

_____

_____

4: What is possession?

Activity 1

Punctuation guide

> The **book** belongs to **Andi**. It is **Andi's book**.

- Possession means that **something** belongs to **someone or something else**. This could mean it is owned by them or is related to them in a different way.
- The **noun that refers to the owner** is in the possessive form.
- A singular possessive noun is made up of the **noun**, an **apostrophe** and then '**s**'.

> Who or what is the owner of each item?

1 Harry's toolbox

_____Harry_____

2 the cat's food bowl

_____

3 Maeve and Stevie's book

_____

Activity 2

Tobias's hand was cold.

- If a singular noun already ends in 's', you add an **apostrophe** and then another '**s**'.

Rewrite each sentence using a noun phrase that includes the words 'owned by'.

1 I read the actor's script.

   I read the script owned by the actor.

2 The firefighter's uniform was red.

   _____

3 Yang liked Claris's parrot.

   _____

4 Charles's food was getting cold.

   _____

Activity 3

Say each sentence **without** using a possessive form.

1 Wednesday's lessons are maths, English and science.

2 We live near our town's biggest park.

3 I enjoyed Neeta's song.

5: Using possessive apostrophes

Activity 1

Punctuation guide

- Possession is a way of showing that something belongs to someone or something else. This could mean it is owned by them or is related to them in a different way.
- A singular possessive noun is made up of the noun, an apostrophe and then 's'.
- If a singular noun ends in 's', you add an apostrophe and then **another** 's'.

Change each phrase to use a possessive noun.

1 the suitcase owned by Martha

Martha's suitcase

2 the football owned by Magnus

_____

3 the hat owned by Jared

_____

Activity 2

Change the underlined words to include a possessive noun.

1 <u>The tallest tree in the world</u> is a redwood.

  The world's tallest tree is a redwood.

2 <u>The aims of this class</u> are simple.

3 I loved <u>the new recipe that the chef created</u>.

4 That picture is <u>the favourite of Chris</u>.

Activity 3

Correct the use of apostrophes in each noun phrase.

1 the suns heat

2 James' cat

3 some green tree's

6: What are contractions?

Activity 1

Punctuation guide

> I can**no**t swim but I **a**m learning.
> I **can't** swim but **I'm** learning.

- **Contractions** are words that have been shortened.
- **Apostrophes** in contractions show where **letters have been missed out**.

Underline the contraction in each sentence.

1 <u>I'm</u> so hot.

2 She can't come.

3 It's a big problem.

Activity 2

Punctuation guide

I **cannot** swim but **I am** learning. **You are** learning, too.
It is hard.

I **can't** swim but **I'm** learning. **You're** learning, too.
It's hard.

- Many contractions involve the words 'not', 'am', 'are' or 'is'.

Complete the table to show what each contraction means.

Contraction	Meaning
I'm	I am
can't	
they're	
she's	
isn't	

Activity 3

Write the sentences using full words instead of contractions.

1 We're late. _____

2 He's running home. _____

3 We haven't got it. _____

7: Using contractions

Activity 1

Punctuation guide

- Contractions are words that have been shortened.
- Apostrophes in contractions show where letters have been missed out.

Add an apostrophe to each contraction.

Full words	Contractions
I am	I ' m
you are	y o u r e
she is	s h e s
cannot	c a n t

Activity 2

Punctuation guide

- Many contractions involve the words 'not', 'am', 'are' or 'is'.

Change the sentences by forming contractions from the underlined words.

1 I want to see you but I <u>cannot</u>.

   I want to see you but I can't.

2 She told me <u>they are</u> here.

_____

3 We <u>do not</u> play outside when it rains.

_____

4 <u>I am</u> on my way home now.

_____

Activity 3

Change each sentence to include one contraction.

1 She practised a lot so she is ready.

_____

2 Make sure he does not rush his work.

_____

What do I Know?

1 I can write statements, exclamations and questions using the correct punctuation marks.

2 I know how commas and the word 'and' should be used in lists.

3 I can include a list in a sentence.

4 I know that a singular possessive noun is formed using an apostrophe and 's'.

5 I can understand what a possessive noun means.

6 I can use an apostrophe and 's' to form a singular possessive noun

7 I can see how apostrophes replace letters in contractions.

8 I can form contractions using apostrophes.

1: What is Standard English?

Activity 1

Grammar guide

| I **is** happy. ✗ | I **am** happy. ✓ |

- Standard English is English that uses correct grammar and punctuation.
- Using the correct **verb forms** is important.

> Underline the error in each sentence.

1 Parissa and I have just <u>being</u> to the park.

2 I were about to tell you my idea – don't interrupt!

3 AJ and Michelle hasn't got time to come out.

4 The postman bringed us the some parcels.

Activity 2

Grammar guide

You and **me** **are** **go** to **sea** each other in **a** hour ✗
You and **I** **are** **going** to **see** each other in **an** hour. ✓

- In Standard English, **spelling** and **punctuation** must be correct.
- All words, such as **verb forms**, **nouns**, **pronouns** and **determiners**, must match up correctly.

Tick the sentences that use Standard English. Underline the parts of the other sentences that are not Standard English.

- Mo took care of his younger sister and her friend. ✓
- Gert gave the whistle to Jennie and I. ◯
- Younger children are not aloud in. ◯
- I watched as the toy sank into the pond. ◯
- The list was simple: I had to get eggs milk cheese and cereal. ◯
- Logan was convinced that his parents were hiding something. ◯

Activity 3

Grammar guide

I'm going to see you later. You're coming to visit me.

- **Contractions** can be used in Standard English, if they are formed correctly.

Circle the **incorrect** contractions in the paragraph.

The plan is this: I'm going to approach the building from the front and you'l approach from the back, looking for guards. The'yre probably going to be inside, where they won't hear us. We'd better make sure there aren't any mistakes: we cant let things go wrong.

2: Using Standard English

Activity 1

Grammar guide

- Standard English is English that uses correct grammar, spelling and punctuation.
- All words such as nouns, pronouns, verb forms and determiners must match up correctly.

Complete each sentence with the correct form of the verb given in brackets.

1 All day yesterday, I ___was___ just lying in the bed. (be)

2 Ethan is planning to share the food he _____ . (have)

3 Rain started to fall. Shi-An _____ she should have worn a coat. (know)

4 I hurried around the corner. "You're late," Martha _____. (say)

Activity 2

Rewrite the paragraph using Standard English.

Frank were looking out of some window at the playing feild we wished he could be out their. Then he was braught back to reality buy his teacher that had noticed he was day-dreaming.

Frank was looking out

Activity 3

Rewrite the paragraph, correcting the punctuation.

This week I've started a? project about bridges at school, this is our second lesson. Mr grays' teaching us to build a model bridge test it and improve it.

What do I know?

1 I understand what Standard English is.

2 I can spot Standard English.

3 I can use correct verb forms, spelling, punctuation and grammar to create Standard English.

Here are some useful meanings. Key terms to understand are in orange.

Term	Meaning
Adjective	Adds information to a noun. It describes what something is like. For example: 'the red dress'.
Adverb	Adds information to adjectives, verbs or other adverbs. Many adverbs end '–ly', but not all of them. For example: 'I ran quickly. I was soon exhausted.'
Agreement	When all of the verb forms, nouns and other parts match together in the right ways, such as in their tenses.
Alphabet	All the letters in order from A to Z. A list of words in alphabetical order starts with letters that come first in the alphabet. For example: apple, ball, cat.
Apostrophe (')	A punctuation mark used to show that letters have been missed out in a contraction. It can also be used to show possession. For example: 'can't'; 'the horse's ears'.
Article	The words 'a', 'an', 'the' and 'some. They come before nouns. They give basic information about whether something is singular or plural and particular or general.
Auxiliary verb	Used to help create different forms of verbs. Forms of the auxiliary verb 'be' are used in progressive tenses.
Capital letter	Large versions of letters. They may also be formed differently. A capital letter is used at the start of a sentence or a name. For example: A, B, C.

Term	Meaning
Clause	A group of words, including a subject and a verb, that means one thing but is not a full sentence.
Comma (,)	A punctuation mark used used to separate items in a list and parts of a sentence that are not two clauses. We often read it as a short pause.
Command	A sentence that gives an instruction. Commands are often exclamations, but never questions.
Compound	When two shorter words are joined together they make a compound word. For example: super + man = superman; play + ground = playground.
Conjunction	Words that link sentences together to form one longer sentence. In the new sentence, the original sentences become known as clauses.
Consonant	Any letter that is not a vowel.
Contraction	Words that have been shortened. Apostrophes in contractions show where letters have been missed out.
Coordinating conjunction	Links two main clauses in a sentence.
Determiner	Determiners, which include articles, come before nouns. They can give basic information about whether something is singular or plural and particular or general. For example: 'two boxes'; 'all of the things'.
Exclamation	A sudden cry that shows surprise, excitement or shock.
Exclamation mark (!)	A punctuation mark used at the end of a sentence to show that the sentence is an exclamation.

Term	Meaning
Expanded noun phrase	A noun phrase that includes extra information about the thing named by the noun, for example using an adjective.
Full stop (.)	A punctuation mark used at the end of a sentence, to show that the sentence is a statement.
Irregular	Words that do not follow rules when they change. Verbs could have irregular tenses. Nouns could have irregular plurals.
Letter	A symbol used for writing. One group of letters makes up one word.
List	A series of connected things. For example: 'In the pond, there are fish, frogs, toads and newts.'
Main clause	Gives the main point in a sentence. There can be more than one main clause in a sentence if they are equally important. If there are two main clauses joined by a conjunction in a sentence, swapping the order of two main clauses does not affect the meaning of the sentence.
Meaning	The thing or idea that a word, expression or sign represents.
Noun	A word that names a person, thing, event or idea.
Noun phrase	A group of words that all link to the thing named by the noun. A noun phrase could be as short as two words: a determiner and the noun.
Object	Something or someone that is involved in the action, but not doing the action. For example: 'Shanice plays the game.'
Past tense	A way of writing a verb to show that events or actions happened in the past.

Term	Meaning
Phrase	A group of words that have meaning. It is not a full sentence, it could be just two words.
Plural	More than one of a thing, or more than one person or thing doing an action.
Possession	Means that something belongs to someone or something. This could mean it is owned by them or is related to them in a different way.
Possessive noun	Shows possession. The noun that refers to the owner takes the possessive form. A singular possessive noun is made up of the noun, an apostrophe and then 's'.
Present participle	A verb tense formed by adding 'ing' (for example: 'sleeping'). Present participles are used to form progressive tenses.
Present tense	A way of writing a verb to show that events or actions happen now or happen regularly.
Progressive	Ways of writing a verb to show that an action continues over a period of time. It is formed by the auxiliary verb 'is' and a present participle.
Pronoun	A word that stands in for a noun or noun phrase. The words 'I', 'you' singular, 'he', 'she', 'it', 'we', 'you' plural and 'they' are all pronouns.
Punctuation	The marks made in writing that are not letters. Punctuation makes writing easier to understand.
Question	A sentence that is used to ask something.
Question mark (?)	A punctuation mark used at the end of a sentence, in place of a full stop, to show that a sentence is a question.
Sentence	A group of words that means one whole thing. It gives a whole idea.

Term	Meaning
Singular	Only one thing, or one person or thing doing an action.
Standard English	Standard English is English that is grammatically correct.
Statement	A sentence that ends with a full stop rather than a question mark or an exclamation mark. It gives a piece of information.
Subject	The person or thing doing an action. The subject carries out the action named by the verb.
Subordinate clause	Gives extra information that is not the key point in a sentence. There cannot be a subordinate clause in a sentence without a main clause. If a main clause and a subordinate clause are joined by a conjunction in a sentence, swapping their positions affects the meaning or makes no sense.
Subordinating conjunctions	Links a main clause to a subordinate clause in a sentence.
Suffix	A letter or group of letters added to the end of a word.
Tense	Shows when the action happens.
Verb	The name of an action. Every sentence must contain at least one verb.
Vowel	The letters 'a', 'e', 'i', 'o' and 'u'.
Word	A group of spoken sounds or written letters that make up one unit of meaning. In slow speech, a word has silence on each side of it. In writing, a word has a space on each side of it.

Answer key

Determiners

1: What are determiners?

Activity 1
some – the
the – a
some – the
a – an

Activity 2
some; the; most of the; many;
several; a few; one; all the
[each underlined]

Activity 3
some: general, plural
the: particular, either plural or singular
most of the: particular, plural
many: general, plural
several: general, plural
a few: general, plural
one: particular, singular
all the: particular, plural

2: Adding information about number

Activity 1
1. some
2. most
3. one
4. no

Activity 2
an; [Children's answers will vary,
but each must be quantifiers
indicating singular (example),
plural, singular and then plural
nouns.]

Activity 3
[Children's answers will vary, but
each must be two sentences and
include 'every', 'plenty of' and 'five'.]

3: Choosing determiners

Activity 1
1. a few of the
2. a / one
3. most / all three / some / many

Activity 2
1. a; one
2. [Two of these options:] most; all
three; some; a few of the; many
3. [Two of these options not
selected for Question 2:] most;
some; a few of the; many

Activity 3
[Children's answers will vary, but
each must be two sentences and
include at least three different
determiners.]

Adjectives

1: What are adjectives?

Activity 1
best; big; older; delicious; blue
[each circled]

Activity 2
1. A tall
2. [Children's answers will vary,
but each must include 'some' or
'the' and an adjective.]
3. [Children's answers will vary,
but each must include 'a' or
'the' and an adjective.]
4. [Children's answers will vary,
but each must include 'a', or
'the' and an adjective.]

Activity 3
[Children's answers will vary, but
each must be two sentences with
at least one adjective in each.]

2: Expanding noun phrases

Activity 1
1. Some clouds [underlined]
2. An aeroplane [underlined]
3. The sparkling raindrops [underlined]
4. a bright yellow raincoat [underlined]

Activity 2
[Children's answers will vary, but each must be two sentences with at least one expanded noun phrase in each.]

Activity 3
[All expanded noun phrases must be written and all adjectives used must be underlined.]

Verb forms

1: Practising the present tense

Activity 1
I play outside. Then the weather gets gloomy. We watch TV instead.

Activity 2
1. cycles
2. carries
3. crosses
4. does

Activity 3
1. cries [underlined]
2. goes [underlined]
3. plays [underlined]

2: What is the past tense?

Activity 1
played [underlined]; finished [underlined]; enjoy [circled]; cleaned [underlined]; fold [circled]; want [circled]

Activity 2
We tidied up. [ticked]
Dana travelled to the city. [ticked]
I stayed at home. [ticked]

Activity 3
We planned a school trip. [ticked]
You enjoyed the concert. [ticked]

3: Using the past tense

Activity 1
1. covered
2. asked
3. helped

Activity 2
Singular: looked; stared; watched
Plural: spied; travelled; stayed

Activity 3
[Children's answers will vary, but each must be two sentences written written using past-tense forms of some of these verbs.]

4: What is verb agreement?

Activity 1
1. Ella and Tom play football.
2. For my party, Mum booked a magician.

Activity 2
[The verbs 'start', 'share', 'played' and 'enjoys' should have been circled.]
1. start – started
2. share – shared

3. played – play
4. enjoys – enjoy

Activity 3
1. played football.
2. [Children's answers will vary, but each must include a third-person singular present-tense verb.]
3. [Children's answers will vary, but each must include a third-person plural present-tense verb.]
4. [Children's answers will vary, but each must include a first-person singular past-tense verb.]

5: Understanding 'be' and 'have'

Activity 1
HAVE Present tense: have, have, has, have; have; have
HAVE Past tense: had; had; had; had; had; had
BE Present tense: am; are; is; are; are; are
BE Past tense: was; were; was; were; were; were

Activity 2
1. have; have; has; have; have
2. were; was; was; were; was; were; was; were

Activity 3
1. [This activity is completed orally. Children should say:]

Every night, I had the same dream. You had a box with two big locks. Your brother had the keys. We had a race to get them. Then we saw that they had broken ends and couldn't be used.

2. [This activity is completed orally. Children should say:]

We are all in the school play. The setting is a dangerous city. Pete is the thief and he robs a bank. You are the manager and Jamala is a police officer. The other pupils are citizens. I am the detective and I stop the thief. You are all very grateful.

6: Understanding other irregular verbs

Activity 1
write; feels; grow; finds

Activity 2
said; went; took; came; saw; knew
got; gave; ran; thought; told; could

Activity 3
began; sang; read; spoke; made; understood

7: What are progressive verbs?

Activity 1
1. am [circled]; going [underlined]
2. is [circled]; pouncing [underlined]
3. was [circled]; feeling [underlined]
4. were [circled]; relaxing [underlined]

Activity 2
Anima was not expecting to win, but hoped she would. [ticked]
wait [underlined]
They are travelling abroad until the end of the year. [ticked]
had [underlined]

Lexi was getting annoyed by Jess's bad memory. [ticked]

Mum coming [underlined]

Activity 3

Anita's jeans were wearing out. – past progressive

Josef's rucksack is too heavy. – simple present

The fair was open all summer. – simple past

Despite the snow, trains are running. – present progressive

8: Using progressive verbs

Activity 1

1. was
2. is
3. were
4. am

Activity 2

1. a. Tara was eating in the cafeteria.
   b. Jon and I were kicking the ball to each other during break.
   c. I was looking everywhere for my school bag.
2. a. Channel 19 is showing my favourite programme today.
   b. I am cooking dinner with Uncle Aarav.

Activity 3

help; run; wait; had; looked [each underlined]

Adverbs

1: What are adverbs?

Activity 1

1. neatly [underlined]
2. playfully [underlined]
3. lots [underlined]
4. loudly [underlined]
5. outside [underlined]

Activity 2

1. heavily [underlined]; verb
2. extremely [underlined]; adjective
3. later [underlined]; verb
4. so [underlined]; adjective
5. almost [underlined]; verb

Activity 3

What happens next? [ticked]

We cross the road carefully. [ticked]

Afterwards, Jo sadly left. [ticked]

2: Adding adverbs

Activity 1

1. suddenly
2. [Children's answers will vary, but must be an appropriate adverb from the bank.]
3. [Children's answers will vary, but must be a different appropriate adverb from the bank.]

Activity 2

1. I answer the question well.
2. [Children's answers will vary, but must add an appropriate adverb from the bank to the sentence 'We play football.']
3. [Children's answers will vary, but must add an appropriate adverb from the bank to the sentence 'I have a maths lesson.']

4. [Children's answers will vary, but must add an appropriate adverb from the bank to the sentence 'We have some free time.']

Activity 3

1–3. [Children's answers will vary, but must add an appropriate adverb to the sentence.]

Conjunctions and clauses

1: Practising 'and'

Activity 1

1. We played games and then we watched a film.
2. I went sledging and Hoonie came with me.
3. I've always wanted a pet and soon I'll get one.

Activity 2

1–3. [Children's answers will vary, but each must be a sentence that links two clauses with 'and'.]

Activity 3

[All instances of 'and' in children's answers to Activity 2 must be circled.]

[Each clause in children's answers to Activity 2 must be underlined.]

2: Understanding 'but' and 'because'

Activity 1

1. but [underlined]
2. because [underlined]

Activity 2

1. The second idea is a reason. [ticked]
2. These are similar ideas. [ticked]
3. These are different ideas. [ticked]

Activity 3

The old man yawns because he feels sleepy. [ticked]
Yan tried to see but it was too dark. [ticked]
Aunt Tabby cooked and I helped her. [ticked]

3: Using 'and', 'but' and 'because'

Activity 1

1. because
2. but
3. and

Activity 2

1. [Children's answers will vary, but each must connect the children's two spoken sentences with 'because' to form one full sentence describing an event and its cause.]

2. [Children's answers will vary, but each must connect the children's two spoken sentences with 'but' to form one full sentence containing contrasting ideas.]

Activity 3

1. because
2. but
3. and

4: Understanding 'or' and 'so'

Activity 1
because; and; or; but; so; because [each underlined]

Activity 2
Bill was early but Elli was late.
– These are very different ideas.
I play with Salib or I play with Jess.
– There are two possibilities.
Dad was annoyed because the train was late.
– The second idea is a reason.
I felt ill so we went to see the doctor.
– The second idea is an effect.
Nish reads his book and he enjoys it.
– These are similar ideas.

Activity 3
1. or [underlined]
2. or [underlined]
3. so [underlined]
4. so [underlined]

5: Using 'or' and 'so'

Activity 1
1. I missed my gran so I went to visit her.
2. We can go swimming or we can play mini golf.

Activity 2
1. [Children's answers will vary, but each must be a sentence containing two clauses expressing two possibilities, linked by 'or'.]

2. [Children's answers will vary, but each must be a sentence containing two clauses describing an action and its effect, linked by 'so'.]

Activity 3
Sam washed the car. Megan helped him. – and
I broke a window. I had to stay at home. – so
Bella could go out. She could stay in. – or
I ate lots of breakfast. I was hungry. – because
The sun is out. The wind is cold. – but

6: Different types of clause

Activity 1
9 / nine

Activity 2
1. We went to a theme park because it was my birthday. [ticked]
   We got there early so the queues were short. [ticked]
2. [Children's answers will vary, but each must be a sentence containing a main clause and a subordinate clause expressing an effect, using 'so'.]

Activity 3
because; so [each circled]

Punctuation

1: Practising sentence punctuation

Activity 1

1. **?** [question mark] [circled]; question
2. **!** [exclamation mark] [circled]; exclamation
3. **.** [full stop] [circled]; statement

Activity 2

1. [Children's answers will vary, but each must be a full-sentence statement.]
2. [Children's answers will vary, but each must be a full-sentence question.]
3. [Children's answers will vary, but each must be a full-sentence exclamation.]

Activity 3

You can help me.
Can you help me?
Help me!

2: Understanding lists

Activity 1

Noun 1: trees
Noun 2: birds

Noun 3: bees
Noun 4: clouds

Activity 2

Get out the milk, eggs, flour and butter. [ticked]
Fruit, vegetables and water are good for you. [ticked]

Activity 3

You need to walk, feed and brush your puppy. [ticked]
Dad baked cookies, scones, cupcakes and muffins. [ticked]

3: Writing lists

Activity 1

coat; scarf; gloves

Activity 2

1–3. [Children's answers will vary, but each must be a correctly punctuated list of three nouns or noun phrases.]

Activity 3

[Children's answers will vary, but each must be a correctly punctuated list of four nouns or noun phrases.]

4: What is possession?

Activity 1

1. Harry
2. the cat
3. Maeve and Stevie

Activity 2

1. I read the script owned by the actor.
2. The uniform owned by the fire fighter was red.
3. Yang liked the parrot owned by Claris.
4. The food owned by Charles was getting cold.

Activity 3

[Children's answers may differ slightly and may be given orally.]

1. The lessons on Wednesday are maths, English and science.

2. We live near the biggest park in our town.
3. I enjoyed the song that Neeta sang.

5: Using possessive apostrophes

Activity 1
1. Martha's suitcase
2. Magnus's football
3. Jared's hat

Activity 2
1. The world's tallest tree is a redwood.
2. This class's aims are simple.
3. I loved the chef's new recipe.
4. That picture is Chris's favourite.

Activity 3
1. the sun's heat
2. James's cat
3. some green trees

6: What are contractions?

Activity 1
1. I'm [underlined]
2. can't [underlined]
3. It's [underlined]

Activity 2
I am
cannot / can not
they are
she is / she has
is not

Activity 3
1. We are late.
2. He is running home.
3. We have not got it.

7: Using contractions

Activity 1
I'm
you're
she's
can't

Activity 2
1. I want to see you but I can't.
2. She told me they're here.
3. We don't play outside when it rains.
4. I'm on my way home now.

Activity 3
1. She practised a lot so she's ready.
2. Make sure he doesn't rush his work

Standard English

1: What is Standard English?

Activity 1
1. being [underlined]
2. were [underlined]
3. hasn't [underlined]
4. bringed [underlined]

Activity 2
Mo took care of his younger sister and her friend. [ticked]
I [underlined]
aloud [underlined]
I watched as the toy sank into the pond. [ticked]
eggs milk cheese [spaces between words underlined]
Logan was convinced that his parents were hiding something. [ticked]

Activity 3
you'l; The'yre; cant [each circled]

2: Using Standard English

Activity 1
1. was
2. has
3. knew
4. said

Activity 2
[Children's answers may differ slightly but must be grammatically correct.]
Frank was looking out of the window at the playing field. He wished he could be out there. Then he was brought back to reality by his teacher, who had noticed he was day-dreaming.

Activity 3
[Children's answers may differ slightly but must be grammatically correct.]
This week I've started a project about bridges at school. This is our second lesson. Mr Gray's teaching us to build a model bridge, test it and improve it.